# UNION PACIFIC 3985

## By William E. Botkin, Ronald C. Hill and R. H. Kindig

# ACKNOWLEDGMENTS

The authors wish to express their sincere appreciation to Kate Botkin for her superb layout and design work; to the distinguished artist, Howard Fogg, both for his encouragement and for creating the magnificent watercolor painting which graces the back cover; to the extremely talented artist, Mike Danneman, for graciously allowing us to reproduce his outstanding acrylic painting on the front cover; to Stephen Lee for his invaluable assistance in providing and verifying factual data; to the Western History Department of the Denver Public Library for providing prints from the splendid Otto Perry Collection; and to photographers Lou DiMattia, Dick Dorn, Victor Hand, Tom Kelcec, A. D. Mastrogiuseppe, Jr., Dale Sanders, A. J. Wolff, and William S. Young for sharing their excellent photographs in order to make our coverage more complete.

FRONT COVER PAINTING:
Two Union Pacific freights roar past one another somewhere on the vast plains of Wyoming; one is powered by a freshly-shopped 3985 in this masterful acrylic painting by Mike Danneman. (Limited edition prints are available from the Colorado Railroad Museum or directly from Rail Art, 14425 Woodland Place, Brookfield, Wisconsin 53005.)

BACK COVER PAINTING:
A winter storm is raging on Sherman Hill as the mighty 3985 pulls a string of empty reefers up number three track in this dramatic watercolor, which Howard Fogg painted especially for this book.


Library of Congress Card Number 85-9929
ISBN 0-918654-36-X

Copyright by the Colorado Railroad Historical Foundation, Inc.
© 1985
All Rights Reserved

Published by the Colorado Railroad Historical Foundation, Inc.
Colorado Railroad Museum
P. O. Box 10
Golden, Colorado 80402

Printed and bound in the United States of America by
Johnson Publishing Company
Boulder, Colorado

# INTRODUCTION

In many ways Union Pacific Challenger No. 3985 is symbolic. It is the largest operating steam locomotive in the United States and is symbolic of the real work horses of our steam fleet at its zenith. The Challengers were overshadowed by the relatively small number of highly publicized "Big Boy" steam locomotives, but the Big Boys never roamed the system as much as the Challengers nor were they as flexible.

Because of their ability to haul a mile of freight cars at sustained speeds, the Challengers kept the Union Pacific Railroad in the forefront of rail transportation during the hectic days of World War II.

They proved equally flexible on the heavy passenger trains of that era, and in fact, were assigned to them on the western end of the railroad on trains to Los Angeles and Portland.

They built the foundation for the high-speed, high-volume service that has become a Union Pacific trademark.

Today 3985 represents our employees' dedication to their craft and their love for steam locomotives. No. 3985 would not be in operation today without the volunteer efforts of our people who are truly symbolic of Union Pacific's slogan, "We can handle it."

John C. Kenefick
Chairman, Union Pacific System

# FOREWORD

The "Challenger" designation was applied by the Union Pacific to the first 4-6-6-4 locomotive ever built, in September, 1936. The name had previously been used for the Union Pacific's highly successful economy passenger train, and for an inn at the U.P.-financed Sun Valley resort area in Idaho.

The engine was largely designed by the railroad's mechanical department, with some assistance from the American Locomotive Company, in the mid-1930's. At that time, newest freight power on the railroad were 88 3-cylinder 4-12-2's, numbered in the 9000 and 9500 series. While these engines were capable of sustained high speeds with freight trains, the long rigid wheelbase restricted them to the main lines east of Ogden, Utah, and Huntington, Oregon, where curves were relatively mild.

At the time the Challengers were being planned, the only articulated engines on the railroad were a group of aging 2-8-8-0's, which were slow-speed locomotives which were used principally on the heavy grades in Wyoming, Utah, California, and Oregon. The proposed 4-6-6-4's would be able to negotiate the sharp curves in the Blue Mountains of Oregon and on California's Cajon Pass, from which the 4-12-2's were banned. Because the Challengers were to be relatively high-speed engines, they could also be used in heavy passenger service if necessary.

The first 40 of the 4-6-6-4's were received in two groups: 3900-3914 in 1936 and the 3915-3939 in 1937. Twenty more, numbered 3950-3969, came along in 1942, in the early months of World War II. Another group of 25, the 3975-3999, were put into service in June, 1943, and the 3985 was one of the engines in this order, bearing construction number 70174, from the Schenectady works of the American Locomotive Company. A final set, bringing the total up to 105 of the 4-6-6-4 wheel arrangement, appeared in 1944. (The original 3900-3939 group had all been converted to oil-burners and renumbered 3800-3839 by this time; so this latest batch was numbered 3930 to 3949, duplicating some of the original numbers.)

The 3985 was a coal-burner during all its years and spent most of its time on the main line between North Platte, Nebraska, and Ogden, Utah, occasionally coming to Denver or perhaps making a trip over the Oregon Short Line as far as Huntington, which was also coal-burning territory. During its many years of regular service, it handled a great many freight trains and a few passenger trains. The 3985 was officially placed in retirement July 18, 1962, although it had not been operated during the preceding five years.

After being stored at Cheyenne for many years (some of the time it was protected from the elements by being placed in the Cheyenne roundhouse), in 1975 it was brought out and moved to a site near the U.P.'s Cheyenne depot and placed on exhibition.

During the next four years, a number of Union Pacific employees became interested in finding out whether the locomotive could be returned to active service. They volunteered to do the work on their own time, and, with the cooperation of the railroad's management, the engine was moved back into the roundhouse in late 1979 for the necessary work.

The work was accomplished over a period of many months, and by early 1981, the 3985 was ready for testing and was steamed up. Short runs were made around Cheyenne, and finally a test run was made from Cheyenne to LaSalle, Colorado. Subsequently it made two longer trips — one to Sacramento, California, and the other to Pocatello, Idaho, and Salt Lake City, Utah. Because the hot cinders and live coals sometimes tended to start fires along the right-of-way, it was decided not to make any more long trips for the present. Based at Cheyenne, it is used occasionally on excursions between Cheyenne and Laramie over Sherman Hill, which is a less combustible area than some other parts of the Union Pacific System.

Barring any major mechanical difficulties, it seems likely that it will continue to be used in this intermittent service for the foreseeable future.

R.H. Kindig
Denver, Colorado

Barely three years old, the 3985 works an eastbound freight upgrade east of Rock River, Wyoming, on August 26, 1946. The combination of the grade and the 68-car train has slowed the Challenger's eastward progress to 18 mph. (O. Perry)

The acrid smell of warm brake shoes mixes with the aroma of soft coal smoke as the 3985 drifts across the high fill just west of Buford, Wyoming. With the long descent down Sherman Hill ahead, the 61-car freight has slowed to 20 mph in deference to the 1.6% downgrade. August 13, 1949. (R. Kindig)

While most of its working career was spent hauling freights, the 3985 did show up in passenger service occasionally. The crew of the 3985 poses beside their locomotive at Evans, Colorado, with the *Pacific Limited*, #23, on March 23, 1946. (R. Kindig)

On a clear November afternoon, the 3985 blasts upgrade near Hermosa, Wyoming, with an eastbound freight. It is eight more miles to the top of the .8% eastbound grade over famed Sherman Hill. November 20, 1949. (O. Perry)

The 3985 rolls a 123-car westbound freight train up the .5% grade at Hillsdale, Wyoming, at 25 mph on August 24, 1957. (R. Kindig)

The .7% grade near Archer, Wyoming, has bogged the 4-6-6-4 down to 20 mph with its 123-car train on August 24, 1957. Apparently the crew of this westbound freight has taken an interest in the photographer who has been chasing the train on a fine summer afternoon. (R. Kindig)

Posed with the 4023, the 3985 is spotted for the members of the NRHS National Convention outside the roundhouse in Cheyenne on September 1, 1963. For several years thereafter, both locomotives were stored outside along with the 2-10-2 5511. In the early 1970's the locomotives were moved inside the roundhouse to protect them from the elements. The 4023 was later moved to Omaha where it is now on display outside the Union Pacific shops. (R. Kindig)

With only a few days of regular service left before storage, the 3985 pounds upgrade at 20 mph near Durham, Wyoming, on August 24, 1957. The 3985 was stored in Cheyenne and was officially retired in July, 1962. (R. Kindig)

In the company of 2-10-2 5511 and 4-8-8-4 4023, the 3985 quietly passes the time away in the Cheyenne roundhouse. December, 1974. (W. Botkin)

From January 22, 1975, until September, 1979, the 3985 was placed on display just west of the Union Pacific passenger depot in Cheyenne. On September 24, 1979, the 3985 was removed from its pedestal by an Ohio Crane in order to begin the physical restoration project. (A. Wolff)

Just over one month since having been taken off its display pedestal, the 3985 shows signs of the initial restoration progress. At this point, the boiler jacketing and lagging have been removed, and work is proceeding on the throttle and front end. November 3, 1979. (A. Wolff)

Some members of the 3985 Committee take time out to pose for a photograph. All members were Union Pacific employees who donated their spare time to accomplish the restoration. From left to right are Steve Lee, Bob Krieger, Tim Grotheer, John Boehner (3985 Committee Chairman), Don Ringstad and Craig Ringgenberg. Tragically, Don Ringstad was killed in an automobile accident in September, 1981. (W. Botkin)

A sight that no one thought would be seen again . . . a Union Pacific 4-6-6-4 under its own steam in the 1980's! On January 17, 1981, the 3985 felt the heat of a coal fire on its grates for the first time in over 23 years. After being "lit-off" at 10:20 am, the steam pressure was gradually brought up to the maximum pressure of 280 psi until the pops lifted. Although the first steam-up uncovered several minor problems, none were associated with the whistle which operated perfectly (the 3985's whistle was taken off the Big Boy 4004 which is on display in Cheyenne's Holiday Park). (W. Botkin)

Steaming softly in the cold night air, the 3985 is illuminated by the glare of flashbulbs as it rests just outside the old Cheyenne backshops on the evening of its first steam-up since restoration. Much work has yet to be done on the locomotive, including application of new lagging and jacketing on the boiler and reinstalling the sand boxes. The entire project from initial idea to break-in run took just over three years, but actual work, counting inspections done while still on the pedestal, took two years. In the course of the restoration process, the 3985 acquired parts from the 838, 3977, 4004, 4023 and 5511. (W. Botkin)

On the morning of its first real test with a train since the restoration was completed, coal is heaped into the huge centipede tender using a clamshell crane. As built, the tender did not have the coal boards which permit the addition of about eight more tons of coal than the rated 28-ton "level full" capacity. March 25, 1981. (R. Hill)

Steve Lee, Union Pacific Road Foreman/Assistant Trainmaster, waits for the highball. Lee is responsible for the safe operation of the locomotive and compliance with all the operating rules of the railroad. In addition, he often is seen at the throttle of the 3985 and 8444 whenever they operate. The array of numbers beneath the "3985" have the following significance: 4-6-6-4 (wheel arrangement), 4 (fourth series of the class), 69 (driver diameter in inches), 21 32 21 (cylinder diameter and stroke in inches), 405 (weight on drivers in thousands of pounds) and MB (stoker type). The indicated 405 weight is actually for an oil-burning 3900. This was later changed to 407, correct for a coal-burning 3900. (W. Botkin)

In preparation for its first test run with a freight train on March 25, 1981, the big Challenger eases onto the turntable in Cheyenne, Wyoming, under the watchful eyes of the members of the 3985 Restoration Committee. (R. Hill)

Under a cloud of coal smoke and steam, the 3985 gets underway in the Cheyenne yard on its break-in run to LaSalle, Colorado. Just to the left of the smokebox is the tower of the Union Pacific's passenger depot, which for years was the tallest building in Cheyenne. (L. DiMattia)

Heading south toward Speer, Wyoming, the Challenger makes light work of the short 14-car test train on its first operation outside the Cheyenne yard since the restoration work was completed. March 25, 1981. (R. Hill)

Looking as good as the day it left Alco in 1943, the 3985 rounds the final curve into Speer, below. Although the date is March 25, 1981, one has only to imagine, and it is 1955 again! (W. Botkin) At Speer, about seven miles out of Cheyenne, the 3985 makes an inspection stop, right. It seems that repeated efforts to blow the whistle were unsuccessful. A closer examination at Speer by the crew revealed that the whistle had vibrated loose at the union causing the linkage to bind. The embarrassing problem is quickly corrected with a large wrench, and soon the locomotive and its short train are off to LaSalle. March 25, 1981. (L. DiMattia)

Racing downgrade on the Denver mainline toward LaSalle, the 3985 rolls under the Interstate 25 highway bridge just south of Speer on March 25, 1981. (R. Hill)

Blackening the skies at LaSalle, Colorado, the big Challenger approaches the end of its southbound test run on March 25, 1981. (L. DiMattia)

Tim Grotheer and Bob Krieger operate the Alemite pneumatic grease gun to lubricate the right front engine's main rod pin at the servicing stop at LaSalle on March 25, 1981. At this point on the break-in run, it was discovered that one of the spring hanger pins on the frame of the locomotive had broken. This was corrected before the historic doubleheader movement with the 8444 to Sacramento the following month. (W. Botkin)

Quietly awaiting its first official public debut on its historic journey to Sacramento with the 8444, the 3985 rests in the Cheyenne roundhouse beside a rotary snowplow in April of 1981. This section of the roundhouse was torn down two years later, and the engine now resides in the old passenger roundhouse between excursions. (W. Botkin)

After being stopped by a slow westbound freight pulling into Lynch siding, the 8444 and 3985 storm west
out of Lynch, Wyoming, up the new line under a canopy of splendid soot. The two UP steam locomotives
are working their way west to participate in the opening of the California Railroad Museum in Sacramento.
April 23, 1981. (W. Botkin)

Interestingly, Challenger 3985 is only about 7½ feet longer than Northern 8444, as this broadside view of both engines illustrates. The rock formations near Rock River, Wyoming, create a scenic backdrop for the two Union Pacific steam locomotives as they head west toward their first night's stop at Green River, Wyoming, on April 23, 1981. (W. Young)

The Union Pacific steam locomotives pull a rather unattractive assortment of equipment as they round the curve into Point of Rocks, Wyoming, on the afternoon of April 23, 1981. The 13-car consist is certainly sufficiently powered to move over the UP at track speed! (W. Botkin)

Spewing a glorious cloud of steam and smoke into the cool morning air, the 8444 and the 3985 blast out of
Green River  on April 24, 1981. (T. Kelcec)

Much to the chagrin of Southern Pacific's management, the 8444 and 3985 put on quite a dramatic show as they ascend the east slope of Donner Pass at Andover, California, on April 29, 1981. The two SP SD-40 helpers add no tractive effort on the climb up Donner Pass. (D. Sanders)

After spending nine days stealing the show at the opening of the California Railroad Museum, the two Alco
alumni head home over Southern Pacific rails at Long Ravine, just east of Colfax, California, on May 11,
1981. (D. Sanders)

Still on SP rails, the 8444 and 3985 with two SP SD-40 helpers roll by West Reno, Nevada, as
they head east for home territory on May 11, 1981. The diesels were used on the movement over
the SP in order to conserve water. (D. Dorn)

A startled herd of cows bolts as the eastbound 8444 and 3985 roar by, trailing two Southern Pacific SD-40's and the UP consist at Verdi, Nevada, on May 11, 1981. (D. Dorn)

Grimy from 23 days and 2289 miles on the road, the 8444 and 3985 charge upgrade under threatening skies at Hermosa, Wyoming, on May 15, 1981. (A. Mastrogiuseppe)

After being held for a westbound freight coming off the new line, the doubleheader drifts downgrade and prepares to swing onto track three at Dale Junction, Wyoming. In late 1982, the junction of the new line, and the old double track mainline was moved about one mile west in order to alleviate the blowing snow problems at the junction's switches. Ironically, the snow problems are equally severe at the new Dale Junction, which is now located along the tangent section of track just beyond the rear end of the train. May 15, 1981. (W. Botkin)

The big, bald face of the 3985 basks in the late afternoon light. From the front, the 3985 looks very much like a Big Boy. The notable differences are the length of the front deck and the number plate: on the Big Boy it is located low, beneath the headlight. (W. Botkin)

On its first solo outing since the break-in run in March of 1981, the 3985 thunders up the old mainline over Sherman Hill on June 16, 1982. Here, on the big fill between Buford and Sherman, Wyoming, the grade has slackened slightly to .8% from the steady 1.6% climb out of Cheyenne. The Challenger is beginning its journey west to Pocatello, Idaho, to help celebrate Pocatello's 100th Anniversary and UP Family Days. From Pocatello, the 3985 will head south to Salt Lake City to pull its first railfan excursions since the locomotive was restored to active service. (W. Botkin)

The early morning sun glints off the flanks of the big articulated in the Green River, Wyoming, yards on June 17, 1982. (W. Botkin)

The Walschaerts type valve gear and massive rods of the front engine unit were designed for sustained speeds up to 70 mph, but could be operated up to 80 mph. (W. Botkin)

Green River lies at the bottom of a "bowl" so that trains leaving in either direction must ascend a grade. However, the grade westbound is heavier at .8%. Here, the 3985 puts on quite a show leaving Green River westbound (between Riview and Peru) despite its light ten-car train. When moving steam locomotives in other than excursion service, the UP "Steam Crew" designs trains which offer the best combination of added braking power and minimal coal and water consumption. The baggage car immediately behind the locomotive is actually the steam crew's tool car which is equipped to handle servicing and most road emergencies. June 17, 1982. (W. Botkin)

Now on the Northwestern District, the Idaho Division of the Union Pacific, the 3985 rounds this beautiful sweeping curve just east of Waterfall, Wyoming, as it heads west towards Pocatello on June 17, 1982.
(T. Kelcec)

With the Preuss Range looming up in the background, the westbound 3985 passes Georgetown siding after a servicing stop at Montpelier, Idaho, on June 17, 1982. (W. Botkin)

Among the festivities at the Pocatello Centennial and UP Family Days celebration was the grand entrance of the 3985 into town with Union Pacific President J.C. Kenefick at the throttle on June 20, 1982. After the celebration, the locomotive heads south just a few miles south of Inkom, Idaho, on June 21, 1982. (W. Botkin)

The snow-capped peaks of the Bannock Range tower over the 3985 as the Challenger races toward McCammon, Idaho, on June 21, 1982. (W. Botkin)

Amtrak passengers traveling on the *Pioneer* seldom get an opportunity to enjoy the handsome scenery south of Pocatello as both *Pioneers* pass through this area in the wee hours of the morning. The 3985 rolls south through the red rocks between Downey and Swan Lake, Idaho, on June 21, 1982. (W. Botkin)

The giant articulated gingerly eases across the curved trestle in Bear River Canyon just a few miles south of Cache Junction, Utah, on June 21, 1982. Visible in the background is Cutler Dam. (W. Botkin)

The Promontory Chapter of the NRHS operated the first public excursion with the 3985. On Saturday, June 26, 1982, the Challenger put on quite a show that wasn't altogether appreciated by some Utah residents. Because of the extreme dryness of the fields surrounding the trackage between Salt Lake City and Provo, the 3985 set many trackside fires as it smokily ran upgrade out of Salt Lake City. In this classic wedge shot, the southbound 3985 pounds up to the top of the grade at Mount, Utah. (V. Hand)

Night finds the 3985 resting between excursions in the yard. The fire has been cleaned, the ashes dumped, and the engine watchman has only to add a little water and coal to the massive boiler occasionally during the night. (W. Botkin)

On its second day in excursion service, the 3985 thunders up the grade at Draper, Utah, as it heads south from Salt Lake City to Provo. The Wasatch Range forms an impressive backdrop for the train. June 27, 1982. (V. Hand)

After spending two days in Laramie for UP Family Days, the
eastbound 3985 races up Sherman Hill at Sherman. Sherman is the
top of the grade for trains using the old mainline. July 11, 1982.
(W. Botkin)

Some members of the UP "Steam Crew" assemble in Laramie for
their portrait. From left to right are Jim Chval (Assistant Power
Coordinator), Tom Stuart (Road Supervisor - Motive Power), Bob
Neeley (General Mechanical Superintendent-Locomotive, now
retired), Craig Ringgenberg (Boilermaker Apprentice), Steve Lee
(Road Foreman/Assistant Trainmaster), Jim Duncan (Engineer-Diesel
Locomotive Design) and Carl Hudson (Boilermaker Apprentice).
July 11, 1982. (W. Botkin)

Once the Union Pacific gave the okay to use the locomotive in fan trip service, both Denver railroad clubs requested the 3985 for future excursions. However, because of the fire hazard that became very apparent on its excursions in Utah, the locomotive was restricted to operation between Cheyenne and Laramie, where there is little to catch fire. Right-of-way fire problems were common along the UP when steam was in regular service. Some 3900's were fitted with netting around the ashpan sides in an effort to reduce the fire problems. (These can be seen in the photo on the bottom of page 6.) This solution was not, however, entirely satisfactory since most of the live cinders came from the stack. With the Rocky Mountain Railroad Club excursion, the westbound 3985 rounds a curve on the new line between Emkay and Lynch on May 29, 1983. (W. Botkin)

The cut west of Perkins is a traditional place to hold a photo runby, and the westbound 3985 is putting on a good performance as it blasts out of the granite cut at MP 551 on the new line, track three, May 29, 1983. (W. Botkin)

The old and new tracks between Hermosa and Laramie are separated by several miles. Until the late 1970's, both lines were single track. A second main was added to the eastbound mainline over the period of 1975 to 1978. While these tracks are signalled for operation in either direction, most eastbounds use tracks one and two as the ruling grade is .8% vs. 1.9% on track three. Smoke boiling out of the stacks, the 3985 slows for a photo stop at MP 556.5 between Forelle and Colores on May 29, 1983. (W. Botkin)

While few roads' articulated steam locomotives had twin stacks, the Union Pacific adopted the twin stack concept with the development of the new series Northerns, Challengers, and Big Boys in the early 1940's. In this broadside view of the 3985, the twin exhaust stacks clearly demonstrate their effect at Colores during an eastbound photo runby on May 29, 1983. (W. Botkin)

The uncluttered front end of the 3985 becomes apparent in this head-on view, left. The headlight is mounted on the airpump and after-cooler shield, which in turn is attached to the frame of the locomotive. This was done so that the headlight shined on the track when the boiler swung out as the locomotive negotiated curves. Cheyenne yard, October 7, 1983. (W. Botkin) While not quite as complex as the cockpit of a 747, the backhead of modern steam power was always an impressive sight. The cab, below, is much the same as when it left Alco in 1943 except for the addition of a speedometer, radio and cab signals. Headphones are used with the radio, since the cab becomes rather noisy when the Challenger is blasting along. (W. Botkin)

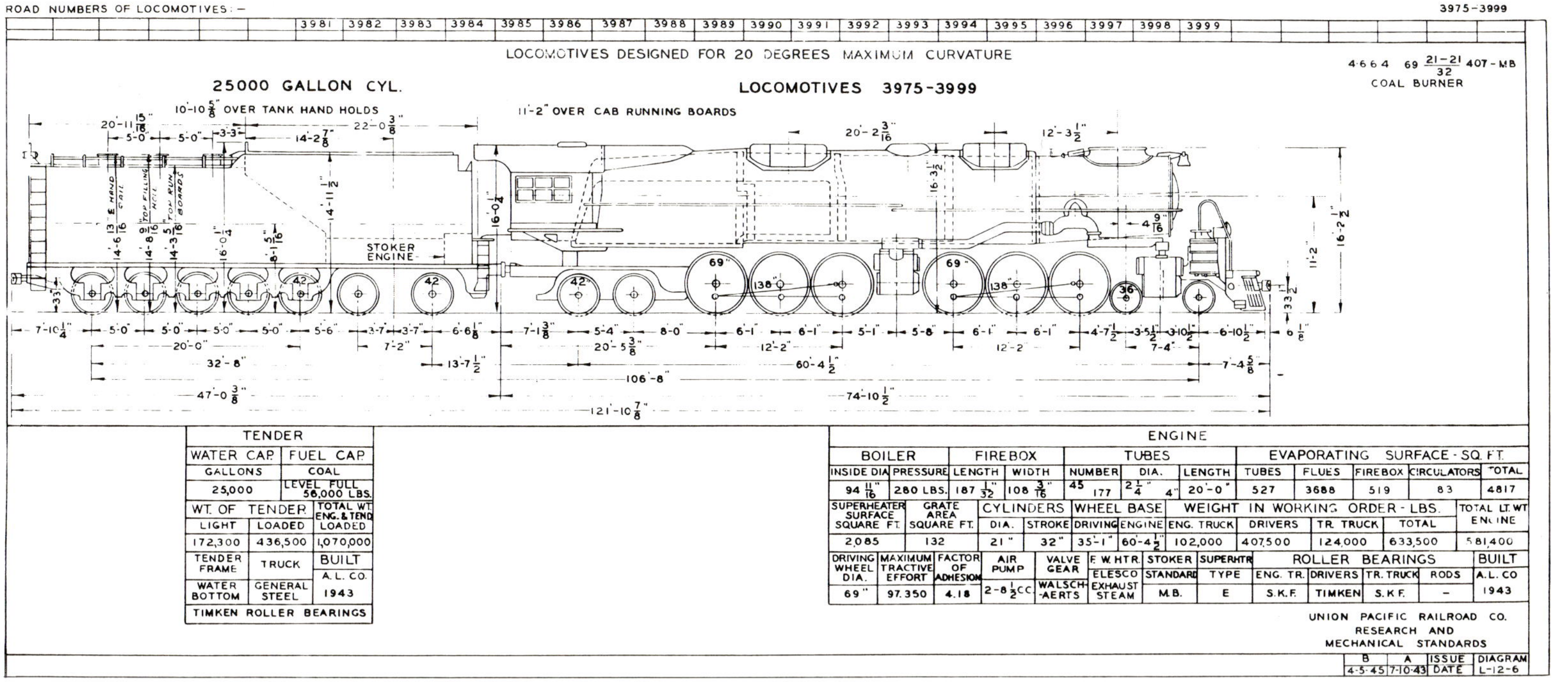

| 3981 | 3982 | 3983 | 3984 | 3985 | 3986 | 3987 | 3988 | 3989 | 3990 | 3991 | 3992 | 3993 | 3994 | 3995 | 3996 | 3997 | 3998 | 3999 |



### TENDER

| WATER CAP. | | FUEL CAP. | |
|---|---|---|---|
| GALLONS | | COAL | |
| 25,000 | | LEVEL FULL 56,000 LBS. | |
| WT. OF TENDER | | | TOTAL WT. ENG. & TEND. |
| LIGHT | LOADED | | LOADED |
| 172,300 | 436,500 | | 1,070,000 |
| TENDER FRAME | TRUCK | | BUILT |
| WATER BOTTOM | GENERAL STEEL | | A.L. CO. 1943 |
| TIMKEN ROLLER BEARINGS | | | |

### ENGINE

| BOILER | | FIREBOX | | TUBES | | | EVAPORATING SURFACE - SQ. FT. | | | | |
|---|---|---|---|---|---|---|---|---|---|---|---|
| INSIDE DIA | PRESSURE | LENGTH | WIDTH | NUMBER | DIA. | LENGTH | TUBES | FLUES | FIREBOX | CIRCULATORS | TOTAL |
| 94 11/16" | 280 LBS. | 187 1/32" | 108 3/16" | 45 / 177 | 2 1/4" / 4" | 20'-0" | 527 | 3688 | 519 | 83 | 4817 |

| SUPERHEATER SURFACE SQUARE FT. | GRATE AREA SQUARE FT. | CYLINDERS | | WHEEL BASE | | WEIGHT IN WORKING ORDER - LBS. | | | | | TOTAL LT. WT ENGINE |
|---|---|---|---|---|---|---|---|---|---|---|---|
| | | DIA. | STROKE | DRIVING | ENGINE | ENG. TRUCK | DRIVERS | TR. TRUCK | TOTAL | | |
| 2,085 | 132 | 21" | 32" | 35'-1" | 60'-4 1/2" | 102,000 | 407,500 | 124,000 | 633,500 | | 581,400 |

| DRIVING WHEEL DIA. | MAXIMUM TRACTIVE EFFORT | FACTOR OF ADHESION | AIR PUMP | VALVE GEAR | F. W. HTR. ELESCO EXHAUST STEAM | STOKER STANDARD M.B. | SUPERHTR TYPE E | ROLLER BEARINGS | | | | BUILT |
|---|---|---|---|---|---|---|---|---|---|---|---|---|
| | | | | | | | | ENG. TR. | DRIVERS | TR. TRUCK | RODS | A.L. CO |
| 69" | 97.350 | 4.18 | 2-8 1/2 CC | WALSCH-AERTS | | | | S.K.F. | TIMKEN | S.K.F. | — | 1943 |

UNION PACIFIC RAILROAD CO.
RESEARCH AND
MECHANICAL STANDARDS

| | B | A | ISSUE | DIAGRAM |
|---|---|---|---|---|
| | 4-5-45 | 7-10-43 | DATE | L-12-6 |

The fourth series of the 3900-class Challenger locomotives, above, included both coal and oil burners. The locomotives delivered at that time included road numbers 3975 through 3999. The series from 3975 through 3984 was converted to oil burners in 1946, primarily to serve Los Angeles and Portland in passenger service. (Union Pacific Railroad Company) The huge boiler on the 3985, below, is almost 60 feet long while the fire-box is 15½ feet long and 9 feet wide. Cheyenne yard, October 7, 1983. (W. Botkin)

Posed beside each other, the two handsome UP steam locomotives bask in the late afternoon sunlight in front of the diesel shops in Cheyenne on October 7, 1983. (W. Botkin)

The Race! For NBC's *Today Show*, the Union Pacific graciously fired up both of its operable steam locomotives and staged a side-by-side runby with the 8444 and the 3985. Just west of the depot in Cheyenne, the two giants roll down the mainline. The next day, NBC's camera crew rode the NRHS excursion to Laramie with the 3985. The television film crew quickly learned all about photo lines when they ventured out in front of the fans at one runby location. October 7, 1983. (W. Botkin)

Rounding the broad curve at MP 540.4, just east of Harriman on the new line, the westbound 3985 puts on a fine performance for the fans of an Intermountain Chapter NRHS trip on October 8, 1983. The open front cylinder cocks were an unexpected addition when they stuck open after starting the engine. While ruining the photograph for the fans, the open cylinder cocks also proved to be a serious operating problem for the crew. Running a steam locomotive with the cylinder cocks open consumes tremendous quantities of coal and water and makes it very difficult to keep up the proper operating steam pressure. (W. Botkin)

By the time the October 8, 1983, NRHS excursion had reached the area around Perkins, the landscape was shrouded in fog and mist. The photo stop at MP 551, just west of Perkins siding, takes on an ethereal quality as the giant locomotive bursts out of the fog and steam on its way west toward Laramie. (W. Botkin)

Virtually all westbound UP steam excursions use the new line, or track three, for the trip up Sherman Hill. The line was constructed in 1952-53 to reduce the ruling grade on Sherman Hill from 1.6% to .8%. This was accomplished by first looping the track around to gain altitude, then constructing several deep cuts and high fills toward the west end of the new line near Perkins and Dale. With a 15-car Rocky Mountain Railroad Club excursion on May 27, 1984, the 3985 works upgrade at 40 mph at Emkay. The siding at Emkay was named after the contractor which built the new line, Morrison-Knudsen (M-K). (W. Botkin)

Less than one mile from Harriman, westbound 3985 thunders by with a Rocky Mountain Railroad Club excursion on May 27, 1984. While the old double track mainline up Sherman Hill is more famous, the new line is actually more scenic with its high fills, deep cuts, and broad curves. This area around Harriman and Perkins is particularly attractive with pine trees dotting the rock-studded landscape. (W. Botkin)

Cab windows still tightly shut, the Challenger makes a smoky exit from Hermosa Tunnel on the westbound portion of a Rocky Mountain Railroad Club excursion on May 27, 1984. The engine is drifting at this point down the .8% grade into Laramie. In service, the 3900's and other big UP power exhibited smoke problems when drifting downgrade because of the huge double stack area. When under load, of course, the exhaust velocity was sufficient to keep the smoke up high enough so that it didn't roll back into the cab. Several 3900's received smoke deflectors, but this was not entirely satisfactory, especially in freight service when the air velocity was rarely great enough to lift the smoke over the boiler. (W. Botkin)

Blasting past the famous rock formation just west of Colores, the 3985 begins to slow for a photo stop for the Rocky Mountain Railroad Club on May 27, 1984. At this point, the Challenger is heading east over the mainline out of Laramie. The westbound main is located several miles to the west. (W. Botkin)

Snow fences dot the landscape on Sherman Hill, but most of the original wooden fences have been replaced with metal ones. Between Colores and Hermosa, several wooden snow fences still exist. The 3985 charges up the .8% grade eastbound with the Rocky Mountain Railroad Club excursion on May 27, 1984. (A. Mastrogiuseppe)

Just west of Hermosa, the 3985 marks its passage with a glorious cloud of soft coal smoke. This eastbound trackage was single track until 1978 when a second track was added to help facilitate traffic movement between Laramie and Hermosa. May 27, 1984. (W. Botkin)

In a full-fledged, raging Wyoming blizzard, the 3985 makes a photo stop for the die-hard fans of the
Intermountain Chapter of the NRHS at MP 540.4, east of Harriman, Wyoming. Unbelievably, the date is
October 20, 1984! (R. Hill)

Once in a while, all of the variables come together exactly right. The first three photo stops on the October 20, 1984, Intermountain Chapter, NRHS, excursion were marred by heavy, blowing snow and poor visibility. However, at MP 551, just west of Perkins, the snow ceased, and the dismal sky brightened. The combination of the snow-covered rocks and pine trees and a great performance by the engine crew resulted in a winter wonderland spectacular. (R. Hill)